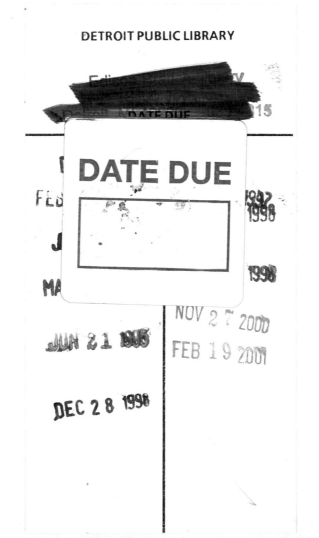

ON THE MAP

JAPAN

Titles in This Series:

Canada	Russia
France	Spain
Italy	U.S.A.
Japan	West Indies

Series editor: Daphne Butler
American editor: Marian L. Edwards
Design: M&M Partnership
Photographs: ZEFA except
Japanese Tourist Office 6t, 23b, 24tr
Spectrum 161, 16br, 23tr, 241, 27b, 29br
Map artwork: Raymond Turvey
Cover photo: *Traditional Japanese dress*

Copyright © text 1993 Steck-Vaughn Company

All rights reserved. No part of the material protected by this copyright
may be reproduced or utilized in any form or by any means, electronic
or mechanical, including photocopying, recording, or by any
information storage and retrieval system, without permission in writing
from the copyright owner. Requests for permission to make copies of
any part of the work should be mailed to: Copyright Permissions,
Steck-Vaughn Company, P.O. Box 26015, Austin, TX 78755

Library of Congress Cataloging-in-Publication Data

Flint, David, 1946–
    Japan / written by David Flint.
      p.   cm.— (On the map)
    Includes bibliographical references and index.
    Summary: An illustrated introduction to the geography, history,
industries, people, customs, and famous landmarks of Japan.
    ISBN 0–8114–2940–7
    1. Japan — Pictorial works — Juvenile literature.
   [1. Japan.] I. Title. II. Series.
DS806.F57 1992
952.04'9–dc20
                                    92–43189
                                    CIP   AC

Typeset by Multifacit Graphics, Keyport, NJ
Printed and bound in the United States
1 2 3 4 5 6 7 8 9 0 VH 98 97 96 95 94 93

JAPAN

David Flint

RSVP

**RAINTREE
STECK-VAUGHN**
P U B L I S H E R S
The Steck-Vaughn Company

Austin, Texas

Contents

Island Country   6–7

Mountains, Rivers, and Coasts   8–9

Volcanoes, Earthquakes, and Typhoons   10–11

Tokyo   12–13

Family Life   14–15

Farming and Fishing   16–17

Food and Stores   18–19

Going to School   20–21

Getting Around   22–23

Sports and Leisure   24–25

Work   26–27

Famous Landmarks   28–29

Facts and Figures   30

Further Reading   31

Index   32

The Seto Ohashi Bridge linking the islands of Shikoku and Honshu opened in 1988.
It carries both road and railroad traffic and is built to withstand most earthquakes.

The city of Kobe is one of Japan's main ports.

Island Country

Japan is a country of islands. Most Japanese live on the four main islands—Hokkaido, Honshu, Shikoku, and Kyushu. From northeast to southeast, these four main islands stretch for about 1,300 miles. In addition, there are over three thousand smaller islands that make up the rest of the country.

The largest island with the most big cities is Honshu. It is sometimes called the main island. North of Honshu is Hokkaido, Japan's second largest island. South of Honshu are Shikoku and Kyushu.

Japan is in Asia, the world's biggest continent. To the west, across the Sea of Japan, are China and Korea. To the east is the vast Pacific Ocean.

Japan is a long, narrow country, so the weather changes greatly from north to south. In the north, there are cold, snowy winters. Summers have short growing season. Although the south gets a few days of snow in winter, it melts quickly. In summer the south is very warm and wet. The growing season is long.

Almost 124 million people live in Japan. Most live in towns and cities on the four largest islands.

Mountains, Rivers, and Coasts

Japan is a very small and crowded country. It is almost the same size as the state of California. Much of the land is covered with steep mountains. Mount Fuji is the most famous of Japan's mountains. It is because of the mountains, that only a small amount of land is level enough to farm.

There are many rivers in Japan, most of which are short and steep. They flow from the mountains and tumble down to the sea. With its 228 miles, the Shinano River is the longest river in Japan.

Most of Japan's people live on the land at the foot of the mountains. Nearly everyone is within one hour's drive to the coast. The Japanese coastline is thousands of miles long. Some parts of the coasts are rocky cliffs. Other parts have long stretches of coarse gravel beaches.

Along the coastlines are many small bays and harbors. They have been made into ports. Ships arrive and depart from these ports each day. Hundreds of small family-owned boats brave the tides to bring in loads of fish and seaweed from the waters.

The city of Nagasaki is built around a bay.

The snow-capped peaks of the Japanese Alps.

The broad river in the city of Hiroshima.

Volcanoes, Earthquakes, and Typhoons

For such a small country, Japan has many natural disasters. There are over fifty volcanoes in Japan. No one knows when one may erupt. The volcanoes form some of the highest peaks in the country.

Every year Japan has over 1,500 earthquakes! Fortunately, most of them are so small that people do not notice them. The country's worst earthquake was in 1923. During that earthquake, most of Tokyo, the capital city, was destroyed. Today bridges and other structures are built to withstand earthquakes. Japanese schools regularly hold drills so children will know what to do if there is an earthquake.

Heavy storms called typhoons strike Japan every year. These storms bring strong winds and very heavy rain. Buildings, streets, and even whole towns and cities are sometimes flooded. The high winds cause great damage to homes and other property.

In spite of such disasters, Japan is a place of great beauty. This is especially true in the countryside. There are rolling hills and high snow-topped mountains. Much of the country is covered with forests.

The typhoon season is in September.

...aper walls in rooms help cut down the ...amage from earthquakes.

The crater on the top of volcanic Mount Fuji.

In Tokyo beautiful gardens are close to tall office buildings.

The monorail train in Tokyo helps people get around the city.

Tokyo

Tokyo is one of the largest cities in the world. It rests on the east coast of Honshu Island. About 13 million people live and work in Tokyo. It is the center for government, banking, and international trade Tokyo is also a big industrial center. A wide variety of products are manufactured here.

Much of Tokyo was destroyed during the earthquake and fire of 1923. But the city was quickly rebuilt. Today there are modern skyscrapers and huge shopping centers. Some of the world's best hotels are found in Tokyo. In the old part of the city there are streets of wooden houses with tiny gardens in back of them.

In the center of Tokyo is the Imperial Palace. It is where the Emperor and his family live. Around the Palace the roads were built like a maze. This was to make it hard for enemies to find the Palace. Today, the grounds of the Palace are a favorite attraction of Japanese and tourists.

Tokyo is a busy and bustling city, even at night. Every street is crowded with people walking around, shopping, or going to one of the many eating places. More movie theaters are found in Tokyo than in any other city in the world.

Family Life

In Japan children, parents, and grandparents often live together in the same house. Houses in the city are small and made of wood. Sometimes the whole family lives in just two rooms. Houses in the country are larger.

Japan is a small country with many people. The growing population has created the need for more housing. The Japanese have built apartment houses so that many people can live in one building. Many of these buildings are over five stories tall.

In most families the father goes to work to earn money. The mother looks after the children and home. This has changed in recent years, and more women are going out to work. Often grandparents look after small children.

Before people enter a Japanese home they take off their shoes. Inside they wear slippers or socks. The floor inside the house is covered with rice straw mats. These mats are called tatami.

In the traditional home, the Japanese sit on cushions or chairs without legs. One low table with a heater is used with quilts in winter.

traditional family meal.

In summer a picnic is a family treat.

ames often involve the whole family.

Mealtime on a farm.

Tuna fish are an important food for Japanese people.

Hillsides are terraced to make more flat land for the farmers.

Farmers use small but powerful machines to harvest rice.

Farming and Fishing

There is not much land for farming in Japan. This is because the mountains cover so much of the country. Most farms are small, many are less than five acres. Yet farmers are able to produce large crops on their small farms. Many farms do not have enough space to raise animals.

Rice is the most important crop. Over half of all farms grow rice. It is grown on any available patch of land, even squeezed between houses in towns. Growing rice is a very hard job. In spring all the fields are flooded. Farmers must work in mud and knee-deep in water. Today, many farmers use machines to help with planting and picking the rice.

Japan has the world's largest fishing industry. It catches more tuna than any other country. It also catches cod, sardines, shrimp, and mackeral. In sheltered bays throughout the country, there are farms where fish are raised. In some places seaweed is even grown for food. Because of its vast fishing industry, Japan can sell seafood to countries around the world.

Although Japan has large company-owned fishing fleets, there are still many small boats. These small, family-owned boats make a living from the sea.

Food and Stores

Japan is one of the leading producers of rice. It is the most important food in the country. Most people eat rice for breakfast, lunch, and dinner. Fish is often eaten with the rice. Sushi is a raw fish pressed on to rice which has been seasoned with vinegar. However, tastes are changing. Young people often eat hamburgers, pizza, and ice cream.

Tea is the main drink in Japan. People drink tea with each meal. Teahouses, where people go to enjoy a cup of tea, are found in every town and city.

While rice, fish, and tea are important, they are not the only foods enjoyed by the people of Japan. Pork, beef, and chicken are eaten in large amounts. Vegetables, such as cabbage, potatoes, onions, and tomatoes, are also favorites. In large cities many people have toast and coffee for breakfast.

The Japanese like their food to be as fresh as possible. They do not like their food canned or frozen. Housewives shop for food each day. They go to markets where fresh fish and vegetables arrive daily. Oranges, grapes, cherries, and other fruit are plentiful in most parts of the country.

The Ginza is Tokyo's main shopping street. It has many big department stores, as well as small shops.

Japan's longest covered shopping mall is in Osaka.

Sashimi is a dish of sliced fish, served raw.

Rice cakes are a favorite at meal times.

This shop sells kites of every size, shape, and color.

Japanese people like their children to wear school uniforms.

Children learn to draw the characters of their language.

The school photograph is a time for best uniforms.

Going to School

In Japan all public schools are free, and students must go for nine years. Some children start nursery school at the age of three. There they begin to learn about computers. All children go to elementary school at five and then spend three years in junior high. At fifteen most students go to senior high.

School begins at 8:30 in the morning and ends at 4:30 in the afternoon. There is a one-hour break for lunch. On Saturday, students attend school for half a day.

Classes have up to 50 students, who all wear uniforms. Elementary and junior high students learn science, social studies, mathematics, and many other subjects. From the age of twelve everyone learns the English language. After school many children go to extra classes, called *juku*, to help them do well on their exams.

Most students attend high school after junior high. There they study many of the same subjects they had in junior high. They also take courses to prepare them for college or jobs. Almost all Japanese students graduate from high school.

Japan has many colleges and universities. Students who want to get in must pass a difficult test.

Getting Around

People are constantly on the move in Japan. They travel by car, boat, train, and airplane. In towns and cities, streets are always crowded with cars. A system of freeways, built in the 1960's, eased matters considerably. But, the number of cars increases each day. In cities, major traffic jams continue throughout the day.

Fumes from cars, buses, and trucks pollute the air. The Japanese government has passed laws to cut down on poisonous fumes. Today, companies are building cars that are more able to meet air pollution standards.

Many people use the subways and trains to get around. Japan has one of the fastest and most efficient train systems in the world. However, the trains are also crowded. During rush hours, railroad workers push people into trains to allow the doors to close.

Japan's Bullet Train is world-famous. If it is more than a few minutes late, half the fare is refunded. Railroad tunnels have now been built to link Japan's four main islands.

All of Japan's major cities have airports. There are also smaller airports where private airplanes can land.

The Bullet Train travels at speeds up to 250 mph on specially built tracks.

Japanese roads are crowded, and traffic jams are common in most towns.

Air travel is important within Japan because it is such a long thin country.

Sumo wrestlers struggle to push each other out of the circular ring.

Golf has become a major sport for millions of Japanese.

The Tanabata festival at the shrine in Kyoto.

The art of flower arranging, or ikebana, needs skill and practice.

Sports and Leisure

Many types of sports and recreation are popular in Japan. Sumo wrestling is Japan's national sport. Millions of people watch the two huge wrestlers. The grand champions, called *Yokosuna*, are national heroes.

Many sports popular in other countries came from Japan. Judo, karate, and kendo are still very important in Japan. But baseball is the most popular sport in the country. All big cities have baseball teams. Over 10 million people each year attend baseball games. In addition, millions watch games on television.

On vacations some people like to relax in pools of hot spring water. Hot springs are usually found near volcanoes. Others might visit the big Disneyland park, or the zoo. Walking in temple gardens is also a favorite way to enjoy leisure time.

Many people like to watch television at home with their family. Hobbies play a big role in Japanese family life. Kite flying, tea ceremony, and flower arranging are but a few of the hobbies people like.

In winter millions of skiers flock to the mountains. Hiking and mountain climbing are also very popular.

Work

People get up early in Japan. Mothers are up before 7 o'clock to fix breakfast and pack lunches. Fathers leave for work at around 7:30, and children are off to school by 8 o'clock. The work day in many industries is very long, with some workers returning home late at night.

For a long time many Japanese worked mainly in farming and fishing. Today, Japan has many factories. They make a wide variety of products including toys, cameras, electronic games, and computers. They also produce radios, television sets, cars, ships, and many electronic devices. These items are sold all over the world.

All of Japan's factories are not large ones. There are many small factories, employing less than twenty people. A Japanese company is like a family. Once workers join they do not usually leave.

Large companies in Japan treat their workers very well. The company provides a home, school, and medical services for its workers. The employees work very hard and rarely go on strike.

Japanese goods are reliable and of high quality. New products are always being developed.

apanese businessmen on their
ay to work.

Designing a kimono is highly
skilled work.

ompany workers have a job for life.
here are strict rules about uniforms.

Japan leads the world in the
electronics industry.

Famous Landmarks

The peace monument in Hiroshima.
The explosion of the atomic bomb in
1945 ended the World War II.

The Imperial Palace in Tokyo.
The Emperor, once looked on as a g
is still treated with great respect.

The colorful center of Tokyo bustles
with life day and night.

Mount Fuji, in the Japanese Alps on
Honshu, is Japan's highest mountain.

Japanese Kabuki theater, with its
brilliant costumes, heavy make-up, and
action-packed drama, is world famous.

The beautiful Gold Pavilion in Kyoto.
This is traditional Japanese architecture
built of wood.

Facts and Figures

Japan-the Land and People

Population:	124,000,000
Area:	145,870 square miles
Length north-south	1,550 miles
Width east-west	250 miles
Capital city:	Tokyo
Population:	8,300,000
Language:	Japanese
Religion:	Shinto, Buddhism, Christianity becoming popular

Main Public Holidays

New Year	January 1-3
Doll Festival (for girls)	March 3
Constitution Day	May 3
Children's Day (for boys)	May 5
Emperor's Birthday	April 29
Tanabata (Star Festival)	July 7
O-bon	mid-August
7-5-3 Festival (children aged 7, 5, 3 dress up in their best kimonos)	November 15

Hours and Money

School Hours:	8:30 A.M. to 4:30 P.M. Monday to Friday
Money:	Yen (Y) 122 Yen = about $1.00

Landmarks

Highest mountain:	Mount Fuji 12,388 ft.
Longest river:	Shinano 228 mi.
Largest lowland:	Kanto Plain near Tokyo
Coastline:	17,200 mi.

National Anthem

Kimigayo (The Reign of the Emperor)

Average Temperatures in Fahrenheit

	January	June
Sapporo (north)	12°F	68°F
Tokyo (center)	41°F	75°F
Nagasaki (south)	45°F	82°F

Further Reading

Books

Davis, James E. and Sharryl Davis Hawke. *Tokyo.* "World Cities"
     series. Raintree Steck-Vaughn, 1990
Downer, Lesley. *Japan.* "Countries of the World" series. Bookwright,
     1990
Tames, Richard. *Journey Through Japan.* Troll, 1991

Audio-Visuals

Videotapes

Japan, color, 16 min. National Geographic Children's films, 1987

Index

buildings
  Gold Pavilion 29
  houses 14, 17
  Imperial Palace 13, 28
  office buildings 12
  skyscrapers 13
  wooden houses 13

cities 10, 25
  Hiroshima 9, 28
  Kobe 6
  Kyoto 24, 29
  Nagasaki 9
  Osaka 19
  Tokyo 10, 12, 13, 18,
  28, 29, 30
coast 8

earthquakes 6, 10, 11
Emperor 13

farming 17
  fish 17
  machines 16, 17
  rice 16, 17
  seaweed 17
  terraced 16
festivals 30
  Tanabata 24, 30
fishing 17
  cod 17
  mackeral 17
  sardines 17
  shrimp 17
  tuna 16, 17
food 17, 18
  fish 18, 19

ice cream 18
pizza 18
rice 18
rice cakes 19
sashimi 19
sushi 18
tuna 16
vegetables 18

goods 26
  cameras 26
  cars 26
  electronic games 26

home 14, 25, 26

islands 7
  Hokkaido 7
  Honshu 7
  Kyushu 7
  Shikoku 7

leisure 24, 25
  flower arranging 24, 25
  ikebana 24
  Kabuki theater 29
  tea ceremony 25

mountains 8, 17
  Japanese Alps 9, 29
  Mount Fuji 8, 11, 29
  volcanoes 10, 11

Pacific Ocean 7

recreation 25, 30
  Disneyland 25
  hot springs 25
rivers 8
  Shinano 8

school 20, 21, 26
  elementary 21
  English 21
  exams 21
  juku 21
  junior high 21
  nursery 21
  photograph 20
  senior high 21
  uniform 20, 21
stores 18
  department stores 18
  Ginza 18
  kite store 19
  markets 18
  shopping centers 13
  shopping mall 19
sports 24, 25

travel 22, 23
  Bullet Train 22, 23
  monorail 12
  Seto Ohashi bridge 6
weather 7
  cold 7
  rain 10
  snowy 7
  temperature 30
  typhoons 10, 11
  warm 7
  wet 7
work 26
  businessmen 27
  company 26, 27
  design 27
  electronics 27
  factories 26